COUNTRY LIFE READERS

FIRST BOOK

BY

CORA WILSON STEWART

FOUNDER OF MOONLIGHT SCHOOLS AND PRESIDENT KENTUCKY
ILLITERACY COMMISSION

B. F. JOHNSON PUBLISHING CO.

ATLANTA   RICHMOND   DALLAS

Windham Press is committed to bringing the lost cultural heritage of ages past into the 21st century through high-quality reproductions of original, classic printed works at affordable prices.

This book has been carefully crafted to utilize the original images of antique books rather than error-prone OCR text. This also preserves the work of the original typesetters of these classics, unknown craftsmen who laid out the text, often by hand, of each and every page you will read. Their subtle art involving judgment and interaction with the text is in many ways superior and more human than the mechanical methods utilized today, and gave each book a unique, hand-crafted feel in its text that connected the reader organically to the art of bindery and book-making.

We think these benefits are worth the occasional imperfection resulting from the age of these books at the time of scanning, and their vintage feel provides a connection to the past that goes beyond the mere words of the text.

As bibliophiles, we are always seeking perfection in our work, so please notify us of any errors in this book by emailing us at corrections@windhampress.com. Our team is motivated to correct errors quickly so future customers are better served. Our mission is to raise the bar of quality for reprinted works by a focus on detail and quality over mass production.

To peruse our catalog of carefully curated classic works, please visit our online store at www.windhampress.com.

WINDHAM PRESS
CLASSIC REPRINTS

Preface

There is an increasing demand for the education of adult illiterates who have somehow missed their opportunity in early life, and also for the better education of adults that have a very limited degree of learning. The city has provided for this need to some extent with evening schools, designed mainly for foreigners. All the textbooks for evening schools have, therefore, been prepared strictly for immigrants and city dwellers. Rural America is coming to realize that there exists a need for education among adults in the rural sections as much as among those in the cities. For this reason moonlight schools, rural evening schools, which begin their sessions on moonlight evenings, have been established and have now been extended to fifteen States. The people attending these schools demand textbooks which deal with the problems of rural life and which reflect rural life, and to meet this demand this book has been prepared. The author has utilized the opportunity when the rural dweller is learning to read to stimulate a livelier and more intelligent interest in such subjects as agriculture, horticulture, good roads, home economics, health and sanitation, and those subjects, which, if taught to him, will make for a richer and happier life on the farm.

For illustrations and suggestions the author and publishers desire to express their thanks to the International Harvester Company, *The Country Gentleman*, The United States Forest Service, Mr. J. E. Barton, State Forester of Kentucky, Mr. Roy French, Prof. G. D. Smith, and Mrs. Cornelia Steketee Hulst.

Suggestions to Teachers

An excellent opportunity is offered in this Reader to introduce profitably certain objects and operations of rural life. If the teacher will utilize this opportunity, it will both give an added interest to the subject and impress the principles of the same. Therefore, the teacher is urged to study these suggestions and to follow them as carefully as possible.

1. The script, following the printed lesson, is designed to constitute the writing lesson of the evening's session, and should be copied at least ten times. The letters in script are intended for additional practice work in copying.

2. In connection with the road lessons on pages 10 and 11, a discussion of good and bad roads would be profitable, this discussion being based on the facts stated in these lessons. For instance, there may be an estimate of time lost and of injury to team and wagon by bad roads.

3. For teaching the banking lesson on page 17, a supply of blank checks should be provided in advance. After the lesson has been read, the checks should be distributed among the students. Then, after a line is read in concert, the action mentioned should be performed by the class. For example, after the class reads, "I write the date," all should write the date on their checks; after reading the next line, they should write the name of the payee.

4. The lessons on fruit will be more interesting if samples of good and bad fruit are exhibited, to show the results of spraying and of not spraying.

5. Make the letter on page 23 a real letter. Have it written to the student's mother or some other relative. After the envelope has been properly addressed by the student, have him stamp it and mail the letter.

6. The lesson on testing seed corn, pages 32-34, should be accompanied by the exhibition of a seed tester and a demonstration of its work. Get a farmer to prepare this in advance, giving time for the corn to sprout, and let him bring the seed tester before the class and explain its use and value.

7. For use in the lesson on page 35 concerning a newspaper, the teacher should have at hand a supply of the latest edition of the local newspaper, and should provide each student with one, and follow the lesson with a brief exercise in reading from it.

8. The lessons on health, sanitation, and reform should be emphasized by discussion.

9. After the voting lessons on pages 53 and 54 have been read, an election should be held. A temporary voting booth can be arranged, election officers appointed, and blank ballots, previously prepared, should be voted. After the voting is over, the ballots that are imperfect should be destroyed; a careful count should then be made of the remaining ballots and the winners announced. The candidates may be chosen from the students present.

10. To impress the forestry lessons, discuss forest fires in the vicinity, their probable origin and cost.

11. Before the lesson about wild flowers on pages 67 and 68 is read, the students should be requested to bring in as many varieties as possible of wild flowers. After reading the lesson, such of these flowers should be named as are known to the teacher and student. A book on wild flowers should be consulted in order to learn the names of others.

[6]

THE MOUNTAIN BROOK

| I | read | can |
| you | write | and |

Can you read?
Can you write?
Can you read and write?
I can read.
I can write.
I can read and write.

I can read and write.

to	let ter	your	moth er
my	name	will	fa ther

Mr. John Gray,
    Rock Hill,
        Ky.

STAMP

I can write.
I can write my name.
I can write your name.
I can write a letter.
I will write to my mother.
I will write to my father.
I will write a letter to you.

I will write a letter to you.

we	book	good	it	Bi ble
at	news	home	the	man y

I can read.
I can read a book.
I can read the Bible.
Can you read it?
I will read the news.
I will read many good books.
We will read at home.

We will read at home.

work	time	wag on	for	this
save	team	friend	is	road

This is a road.
It is a good road.
It will save my time.
It will save my team.
It will save my wagon.
The good road is my friend.
I will work for the good road.

I will work for the good road.

bad	rid	see	hurt
foe	of	get	waste

See this bad road !
It will waste my time.
It will hurt my team.
It will hurt my wagon.
The bad road is my foe.
I will get rid of the bad road.

I will get rid of the bad road.

| fat | stock | cat tle | raise | hard |
| are | scrub | mon ey | eas y | make |

See my fat cattle!

My cattle are good stock.

It is easy to make good stock fat.

It is hard to make scrub stock fat.

It is a waste of time and money to raise scrub stock.

It is a waste of time and money to raise scrub stock.

si lo

wood

store

keep

feed

juice

moist

stone

green

fod der

This is a silo.

We can make a silo of wood.

We can make it of stone.

In it we store feed for cattle.

Green fodder is stored in the silo.

The silo keeps the juice in the fodder.

It keeps the fodder moist.

This moist fodder is good for cattle.

them   from   milk   like   have
build   dry   give   does   much

We feed the cattle from the silo.

We feed them the moist fodder.

The cattle like it and it does them good.

Moist fodder makes the cattle fat.

It makes the cows give milk.

Dry fodder will not make cattle as fat as moist fodder.

It will not make the cows give as much milk.

I like fat cattle.

I like to have much milk.

I will build a silo.

I will build a silo.

John	years	old	new	bought
a go	looks	six	un der	shel ter

See this wagon!
John bought it a year ago.
It looks like an old, old wagon.
John does not keep it under shelter.
I bought my wagon six years ago.
It looks as good as new.
I keep it under shelter.
Keep your wagon under shelter.

Keep your wagon under shelter.

all
bank
pigs
hens
coop

pen
barn
hors es
place
things

This is a bank.
It is a place to keep money.
I keep my hens in the coop.
I keep my horses in the barn.
I keep my pigs in the pen.
I keep all my things in place.
A bank is the place to keep money.
I will keep my money in bank.

I will keep my money in bank.

check   a mount   now   fig ures   sign
what   words   that   cor rect   date

I have my money in the bank.

Now I will write a check for my father.

I write the date.

I write the name of my father.

I write the amount of money in figures and in words.

I write what it is for.

I sign my name.

Now I will read my check to see that it is correct.

tree   fruit   why   ripe   poor
full   farm er   but   small   spray

Look at this tree!

It is full of fruit.

The fruit is ripe, but it is small and poor.

Why is this fruit not good?

The farmer does not spray the trees.

Trees that are not sprayed have small, poor fruit.

Trees that are not sprayed have small, poor fruit.

large	sell	here	so
price	fine	right	his

Here is a tree full of fruit.

The fruit is large and fine.

The farmer can sell it at a good price.

What makes his fruit so fine?

The farmer sprayed the tree at the right time.

I will spray my fruit trees and raise fine fruit.

I will spray my fruit trees and raise fine fruit.

Brown	know	care	he
pays	takes	tell	how

Farmer Brown raises good fruit.
Do you know how he does it?
I will tell you.
He sprays all his fruit trees.
He takes good care of them.
That is why he has fine fruit.
It sells at a good price.
It pays Farmer Brown to spray his fruit trees.

Jones	low	ver y
shall	wise	fool ish

Farmer Jones does
not raise good fruit.

Do you know why?

He does not spray his trees.

He has very poor fruit.

It sells at a low price.

It does not pay to raise poor fruit.

Shall I be foolish like Farmer Jones
or wise like Farmer Brown?

I will be wise like Farmer Brown.

*I will be wise like Farmer
Brown.*

tax es   crime   where goes schools
oth er   down   land   glad dis ease

_____

I shall pay my taxes.
I pay a tax on my home.
I pay a tax on my land.
I pay a tax on my cattle.
I pay a tax on my money.
I pay a tax on many other things.
Where does this money go?
It goes to keep up the schools.
It goes to keep up the roads.
It goes to keep down crime.
It goes to keep down disease.
I am glad that I have a home to
pay taxes on.

I am glad that I have a home to pay taxes on.

Barren Fork, Ky.,
Sept. 5, 1915.

Dear Mother:

I have learned to read and write. I am writing you my first letter. This is written in the moonlight school. In this school grown men and women learn to read and write.

I hope to write you many letters and to read many from your dear hand.

With much love,
Your son,
William Read.

house　　neat　　nice　　lives　　fam i ly
peo ple　yard　　say　　clean　　flow ers

This is a nice house.

It is neat and clean.

The yard is clean and has flowers in it.

People that go down this road say:

"A nice, neat family lives in this house.

We know the family from the house that it lives in."

A nice, neat family lives in a nice, neat house.

ug ly	yes	dirt y	paint
la zy	needs	shift less	weeds

"This place is dirty and ugly.
The house needs paint.
The yard is full of weeds.
A lazy, shiftless family lives here."
"Yes, but how do you know that?"
"I know it from the house.
Lazy, shiftless people live in dirty,
ugly homes."

*Lazy, shiftless people live
in dirty, ugly homes.*

| yarn | ball | sky | no | ba by |
| blue | col or | red | eye | ba by's |

"What color shall I paint my house? Shall I paint it red?"

"No, red is for the barn and the ball of yarn."

"What color shall I paint my house? Shall I paint it blue?"

"No, blue is for the sky and the baby's eye."

| gray | then | seen | tan | taste |
| soft | show | white | use | there |

"What color shall I paint my house? Shall I paint it green?"

"No, the trees are all green, and the house will not be seen."

"What color, then, shall I paint my house? Tell me what colors you like."

"I like white. Then there are many soft colors that you can use. There are tan, gray, and brown."

"I will show my taste by painting my house a soft color."

I will show my taste by painting my house a soft color.

club   last   mem ber   girls   she
Jane   crop   to ma to   prize   her

This is Jane and her tomatoes.

She is a member of the Tomato Club.

All the girls in the school are members of the Club.

Last year Jane raised a fine crop of tomatoes.

The crop was so large that she got a prize.

plowed   seed   well   came   box
plant ed   were   some   a gain   soil

Jane planted tomato seed in a box.

The box was full of fine soil.

The seed came up and there were many tomato plants in the box.

Her father gave her some land and plowed it for her.

She planted the tomato plants in this land.

She worked them well.

The crop was very large.

It was so large that the Club gave her a prize.

She is working for the prize again.

My girl shall be a member of a tomato club.

field   him   boys
corn   son   a cre

This is my son John in his field of corn.

He is a member of the Corn Club.

All the boys in the school are members of the Club.

Last year I gave John an acre of land.

He raised a good crop of corn.

The Club gave him a prize.

| kept | ten | yield ed | grass |
| when | fall | dol lars | grow |

John plowed the acre of land.

In it he planted good seed corn.

When it came up, he worked it well.

He did not let weeds or grass grow in his field.

He kept the land fine and soft.

In the fall the corn was ripe.

It yielded a fine crop.

The Club gave John a prize of ten dollars.

He is working for the prize again this year.

I will work for a prize.

want	go ing	each	one
ears	ought	stalk	two

It is time to plant corn.

I am going to plant my corn.

I want to have one or two good stalks in each place.

I want them to grow well and to yield good corn.

I ought to have two ears on each stalk.

come	test	three	made	these
must	stand	third	grains	on ly

I will plant two grains in each place.

But sometimes many grains planted do not come up.

Sometimes they come up, but do not yield corn.

We see in a field many stalks that have not an ear on them.

Where there is a poor stand or stalks that do not have ears, there cannot be a full crop.

If one third of my seed yields no corn, I will have only two-thirds of a crop.

How can I get a full yield?

I must have seed from corn that made a good yield.

I will get seed from corn that had two ears to the stalk.

Then I will test my seed corn.

I will test three grains from each ear.

If these do not come up, I will not plant corn from that ear.

These are the things I must do to have a good yield of corn:

1. I must get seed from corn that yields well.

2. I must test my seed.

3. I must plant it on good land.

4. I must work it well.

I will test my seed corn.

buy   man   should   news pa per

This man is reading a newspaper.
It tells him where to buy.
It tells him when to sell.
It keeps him up to date.
I need to know where to buy.
I should know when to sell.
I want to be up to date.
I will take a newspaper and read it.

I will take a newspaper and read it.

hill   a way   runs   poor er   part
mud   brook   lit tle   rich est   done

"Look at the little brook!
It runs down the hill.
See, it is full of mud."
"Yes, it is taking away soil.
The mud in the brook is made up
of the richest part of the soil.
The land gets poorer and poorer.
It will not raise a good crop."
"What can be done?"

stop	gul lies	sow	brush
fill	pas ture	could	steal

"Run and tell the farmer that the brook is stealing his soil."

"The farmer knows it."

"Then why does he not come and stop it?"

"The farmer is too lazy and shift-less. With care he could keep his soil.

He could sow this hill in grass and use it as a pasture.

He could plant trees here.

He could fill these gullies with brush.

There are many ways to stop the brook from stealing soil.

No brook shall steal my soil."

No brook shall steal my soil.

wore	if	same	may
worn	out	aft er	tried

"This is a poor farm.

It is run down and the soil is worn out."

"What wore out the soil?"

"The farmer raised the same crop on it year after year."

"Could he have saved the soil?"

"He could if he had tried."

"Tell me how so that I may save my soil."

ro tate   mean   first   bet ter

dif fer ent   long   four   be fore

"Rotate your crops and it will save your soil."

"What do you mean when you say rotate your crops?"

"I mean you must not plant the same crop in a field year after year.

You must plant a different crop each year for three or four years. In this way you can save your soil and make better crops."

"Then how long will it be before I can plant the first crop again?"

"You can plant the first crop after three or four years."

"I see! I will rotate my crops."

I will rotate my crops.

| such | learned | wet | helps |
| deep | mois ture | big | turns |

"How does Farmer Brown raise such big crops?"

He gets good seed and tests them.

He rotates his crops.

He plows his land well and deep.

In this way he turns under the weeds and grass.

Land that is plowed deep will hold moisture.

The moisture helps the plants to grow.

Farmer Brown has learned how and when to plow his land.

When it is too wet or too dry, he does not plow it.

I will plow my land well.

THE PLOWMAN   [41]

| cot ton | cloth | oil | food |
| fi ber | thread | rope | South |

Cotton grows in the South.

The fiber of cotton is used to make cloth, thread, and rope.

Its seed is used as food for cattle and to make oil.

A good cotton crop makes times easy in the South.

A poor cotton crop makes times hard in the South.

de stroys   boll   burned
rip ens   ear ly   wee vil

The boll weevil destroys much cotton.

The farmer can get rid of boll weevil by hard work.

Here are some of the things he should do:

In the fall, the weeds and old cotton stalks should be burned.

The land should be plowed deep.

The cotton should be planted early.

Seed from cotton that ripens early should be planted.

The crop should be worked well.

I will do these things and get rid of boll weevil.

I will get rid of boll weevil.

Stony Creek, Ala.,
Sept. 10, 1915.

Dear Father:

A few days ago I wrote to mother. I am still in school and can write better. I am not going to stop until I can write as well as my teacher.

I found it easy to learn to read and write. I wish everyone could have a chance to learn.

Your daughter,
Julia Wright.

ev er y   ache   de cay   meal

tooth brush   pain   teeth   cost

See my new toothbrush!

It did not cost much, but it will save me money.

It will save me from pain.

If I use it after every meal, my teeth will not decay.

If my teeth do not decay, they will not ache.

If I take care of them, I shall not have to buy new ones.

I will brush my teeth and save them.

I will brush my teeth and save them.

skin   fresh   bath   day   dirt
just   sweet   holes   wish   sieve

"How fresh and sweet you look!"

"I have just had my bath. I take a bath every day."

"Why do you do that?"

"It keeps my skin clean. The skin is full of little holes, like a sieve.

In one day dirt can stop up these little holes.

If you wish to feel well, your skin must be kept clean."

show er   sponge   pour   tub
al ways   seems   stream   kind

"What kind of a bath do you take?"

"Sometimes I take a sponge bath. I use a sponge and water to clean my skin.

Then again I take a shower bath. I let the water pour down over me.

Again I take a bath in the bath tub or in the stream."

"It seems to do you much good. Your skin has a good color, and you always look fresh and well."

"Yes, I must have my bath every day; it keeps me well."

"I will take a bath every day."

I will take a bath every day.

fly  dead

filth slops

bring sick

ta ble been

Here you are, Mr. Fly.

I know where you have been.

You have been in all kinds of places.

You have been to the pig pen and to the cattle pen.

You have been to the slops from the sick man.

You have been feeding on a dead dog.

Now you have come to bring the filth from all of these things to my table.

spoil	put	but ter	meat	cooked
drop	kill	din ner	soup	bread

I know what you will do with this filth.

You will drop it into my soup.

You will put it in the baby's milk.

You will put it on my bread.

You will put it on my butter.

You will drop it on the meat that I have cooked for dinner.

If I let you live, you will spoil our food.

And if we eat it, we may all be sick.

What shall I do?

I will kill you, Mr. Fly.

I will kill you, Mr. Fly.

bed   o pen   child   cot   strong
pure   win dow   night   air   ever

"This little child is going to bed.
See the open window by his cot."

"Yes, I see it. Will not the night
air make the child sick?"

"No, the pure night air will make
him grow.

It will make him strong and well.
No one has ever been made sick
by good, fresh air."

sleep ers   breathe   smell   closed
be came   bed room   foul   a fraid

"Some people are afraid to have their windows open.

They are afraid that the night air will make them sick.

Did you ever go into a closed bed-room where there were two or three sleepers? Did you not smell the foul air?"

"Yes, what made the air foul?"

"As the windows were closed, the pure air could not get in.

The sleepers breathed the same air over and over again; it soon became foul."

"I will keep my windows open and breathe pure air."

polls	fold	stamp	e lec tion
mark	vote	bal lot	of fi cers

The polls are open.

I must go in and vote.

I will tell you how I vote.

First I get a ballot.

Then I mark or stamp it correctly.

I fold the ballot and give it to the election officers.

They put it in the ballot box.

Then I have voted.

rules	af fairs	hon or	best
cheats	coun try	him self	voice

With his vote a man rules.

The man who does not vote has no voice in the affairs of his country.

He cheats his country, his family, and himself.

Every man should make use of his right to vote.

He should always vote for the best man or for the one who stands for the best things.

The man who sells his vote sells his honor.

The man who sells his vote sells his honor.

Buck Creek, Tenn.,
Sept. 15, 1915.

Dear Sister:

It gives me much joy to write to the folks at home and to read their letters.

Our moonlight school is still in session. There are many men and women in the school. All of them have learned to read and write.

We study reading, writing, spelling, arithmetic, farming, and history. The study I like best is reading.

We are going to form a

health league and a good
roads club. The league will
work for better health and
longer life. The club will
aid in making roads better.

We are also planning to
have a library. All of us
feel the need of good books.

I wish you were here to
go to school with me. You
must have a moonlight
school in your county.
Then you can go to school.

With love to all, I am

Your sister,

Sallie Spell.

wife
more
pipe
than

buck et
thou sand
sev en
break

"How many buckets of water does your wife bring to the house in a year?"

"Let me see; she brings six or seven a day. That would make more than two thousand in a year."

"Will she not break down?"

"Yes, she may. She is not well.

I will pipe water into my house and save my wife."

I will pipe water into my house and save my wife.

boiled   beans   roast ed   pud ding
stewed   fried   pick led   hom i ny

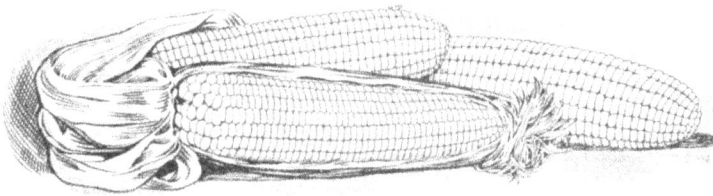

Corn can be cooked in many ways.

It can be roasted on the cob.

It can be boiled on the cob.

It can be cut from the cob and made into soup.

It can be stewed or fried.

It can be made into hominy.

It can be cooked with beans.

It can be pickled.

It can be made into pudding.

Corn is one of our best foods.

Corn is one of our best foods.

hoe cake   gru el   bat ter   pone
dodg er   spoon   muf fin   mush

Corn meal can be used in many ways.

It can be made into gruel.

It can be made into mush.

But the best use for corn meal is to make bread. I will name six kinds that I can make:

Pone, hoecake, muffin, batter cake, corn dodger, and spoon bread.

You can soon learn to make these kinds of bread.

I will not make bread the same way every day.

I will not make bread the same way every day.

di gest   try   change   bake
u su al ly   true   al so   broil

"How do you usually cook meat?"

"I fry it three times a day. That is such an easy way to cook it."

"Yes, that is very true; but fried meat is hard to digest."

"Can you tell me a better way to cook it?"

"Yes, you can roast, broil, or bake it; you can also boil or stew it.

Any of these ways is better than to fry it for each meal. Try some of them for a change."

"I will do so. I will not fry the meat every time."

I will cook meat many ways.

yeast   week   of ten   with out

light   mash   nev er   po ta toes

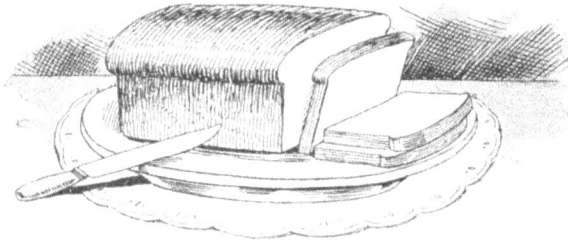

"How good the bread looks! How often do you make it?"

"I make it every week; don't you?"

"No, I never make light bread. I have no yeast. You cannot make light bread without yeast."

"I am going to make some yeast cakes and I will give you some. Then you can always have yeast.

I will tell you how I make it.

I mash two hot potatoes.

hours half luke warm   sug ar
till   pint ta ble spoon fuls   which

"I pour two tablespoonfuls of sugar over them.

Then I pour in one pint of boiling water in which potatoes have been cooked. When this gets lukewarm, I add one yeast cake.

I keep this in a warm place for some hours, till it is light.

I use one cup of this yeast to make bread.

I put the other in a cool place. It keeps a week and I use it, in place of an yeast cake, to make new yeast.

Good bread is more than half of a good dinner."

"Bread is the staff of life."

God   sus tain   would   wom an

God made man.
Woman makes bread.
It takes the bread
That woman makes,
To sustain the man
That God made.
But the bread
That some women make,
Would not sustain any man
That God ever made.

The bread that some women make would not sustain any man that God ever made.

noth ing   eat en   hear

pre pare   please   plan

"Did you ever hear of a dinner made up of nothing but corn?"

"No; did you ever eat one?"

"Yes, I have eaten a corn dinner and I know how to cook it."

"Please tell me how to prepare such a meal."

"I must tell you first the plan of a good dinner. You know all wise cooks plan their meals before they begin to cook."

rel ish   thank

des sert   ____   veg e ta bles

"A good dinner has a soup, a rel-ish, two or three vegetables, and a dessert. Now we can have each of these made of corn.

First we will have corn soup.

As a relish we will have corn pickle.

For bread we will have hoecakes.

For vegetables we will have hom-iny and corn cooked on the cob.

For dessert we will have corn pud-ding."

"Thank you for your plan. I will cook corn many ways, but I do not care to eat a corn dinner."

I will cook corn many ways.

chil dren   tire   heard   who

"How good potatoes are! My children never tire of them. They eat potatoes three times a day."

"So do my children; potatoes are a good food when well cooked."

"I cook them every day; but I cook them a different way each day in the week."

"Seven different ways! Who ever heard of cooking potatoes in so many ways? Please tell me what they are."

jack ets   Wednes day   Sat ur day
Mon day   Thurs day   Sun day
Tues day   Fri day   sal ad

"Here are the ways that I cook potatoes:

I boil them in their jackets on Monday.

I bake them on Tuesday.

I mash them on Wednesday.

I roast them on Thursday.

I make potato cakes on Friday.

I make potato soup on Saturday.

I make potato salad on Sunday."

"My, that is fine! I will try your plan.

I will cook potatoes many ways."

I will cook potatoes many ways.

walk  bloom

wild en joy

woods scarce. ly

"You have been in the house all day. Please come with me and take a walk in the fresh air. It will do you good."

"Thank you very much. I shall be glad to go with you."

"The wild flowers are in bloom. I enjoy them when I walk in the fields and woods; don't you?"

"No, I do not. I scarcely see them when I go walking."

love	joy	missed	life
near	nod	an oth er	smile

"Have you never learned to know the wild flowers and to love them?"

"No, I scarcely know one from another. I only know that one flower is red and another blue."

"Then you have missed half the joy of country life.

I know and can name all the wild flowers near my home. They nod and smile at me as I go by, and I nod and smile at them."

"How you must enjoy them! I will learn their names, too. Then I can enjoy them."

I will enjoy wild flowers.

rob   an y one   rob bers

"What kind of plants are these?"

"They are robbers."

"No, they are not robbers; they are weeds."

"Ah! but weeds are robbers."

"How do weeds rob anyone?"

"They rob the farmer; they steal the land where crops should grow.

They rob the plants of room and light and of food and moisture."

"Then I will get rid of weeds."

I will get rid of weeds.

for est   shade   rain   win ter
beau ty   soaks   winds   sum mer

What a fine forest!

What good shade it makes!

See how large some of the trees are! They must have been growing many, many years.

We must not destroy the forest.

It keeps off the winds.

It soaks up a part of the rain that falls here.

It gives beauty to this place.

In summer it gives us shade to keep us cool.

It gives us wood to keep us warm in winter.

We could not do without the forest.

THE FOREST

pre vent   cause   heat   cold
cli mate   floods   spring blow

If we cut down the forest, it would cause our climate to change.

It would cause cold winds to blow in winter.

It would make the air hot and dry in summer.

It would cause floods in spring.

The soil would be washed away.

It would make this place ugly.

We need the forest to prevent winds, heat, and floods. We need it for its shade and beauty.

I will not cut down the forest.

I will not cut down the forest.

| tim ber | own er | loss | fire |
| lum ber | worth | lose | great |

Look! the forest is on fire.

The good timber is being burned.

Each tree is worth many dollars.

The owner will lose much money.

We say that it is a great loss when one house burns.

The lumber for many houses burns in one forest fire.

Let us put out the fire.

Let us put out the fire.

la bor   less   young
high er   men   wag es

"We have put out the forest fire."

"Yes, but the loss has been very great.

Much fine timber has been burned.

Many young trees have been killed.

The loss of forests makes timber higher in price.

As there is less timber to cut, men who labor will lose wages."

wrong   hunt er   left   care less
think   start ed   built   pro tects

———

"The one who started this fire did very wrong. Do you not think so?"

"Yes; who could it have been?"

"It may have been some hunter. He may have built a fire and left it burning."

"Would a hunter destroy the forest from which he gets food and shelter? He would not be so careless."

"Some farmer may have been burning brush near the forest."

"Would a farmer destroy the forest which saves his soil and protects his home? Every farmer knows that if he starts a fire he ought to see that it is put out."

nuts   rath er   spark   per son
e ven   rail road   train   sure ly

"It may have been started by children who came to get nuts."

"Surely children would not destroy the forest from which they get nuts. Even a child ought to know better than to start a fire in the forest."

"It could have been started by a spark from the train. The railroad is near by."

"That may be true. I would rather think that the fire was started in that way. I do not wish to think any person would be so careless. No one has any right to burn a forest.

We must protect the forest."

We must protect the forest.

Saltville, N. C.,
Oct. 20, 1915.

My Dear Brother:

In my letters from time to time, I trust that you have seen that my writing is improving. I write some each day, so that I may not get out of practice.

You asked why we called our school a moonlight school. We gave it that name because the sessions always begin when the moon shines bright; this tempts men and women from their homes; it also lights them safely over the roads to the school. After we have been to school for awhile, we like it; then we come whether the moon shines or not.

Everyone in this district can now read and write. We are going to keep up the good work. If anyone moves in who cannot read and write, we will give him a chance to learn.

With much love, I am

Your brother,

John White.

FROM THE SERMON ON THE MOUNT

And Jesus said:

Ye shall know them by their fruits. Do men gather grapes of ·thorns, or figs of thistles?

Even so every good tree bringeth forth good fruit; but a corrupt tree bringeth forth evil fruit.

A good tree cannot bring forth evil fruit; neither can a corrupt tree bring forth good fruit.

Every tree that bringeth not forth good fruit is hewn down and cast into the fire.

Therefore, by their fruits, ye shall know them.

By their fruits, ye shall know them.

MATTHEW VII

PARABLE OF THE GROWING SEED

So is the kingdom of God, as if a man should cast seed into the ground; .

And should sleep and rise night and day, and the seed should spring and grow up, he knoweth not how.

For the earth bringeth forth fruit of herself; first the blade, then the ear, after that the full corn in the ear.

But when the fruit is brought forth, he putteth in the sickle, because the harvest is come.

For the earth bringeth forth fruit of herself.

MARK IV

PARABLE OF THE MUSTARD SEED

Whereunto shall we liken the kingdom of God? Or with what shall we compare it?

It is like a grain of mustard seed, which, when it is sown in the earth, is less than all the seeds that be in the earth.

But when it is sown, it groweth up and becometh greater than all herbs; and it shooteth out great branches; so that the fowls of the air may lodge under the shadow of it.

It groweth up and becometh greater than all herbs.

MARK IV

PARABLE OF THE SOWER

Behold a sower went forth to sow;

And when he sowed, some seed fell by the way side, and the fowls came and devoured them.

Some fell upon stony places where they had not much earth; and forthwith they sprung up because they had no deepness of earth.

And when the sun was up, they were scorched; and because they had no root, they withered away.

And some fell among thorns, and the thorns sprung up and choked them.

But others fell into good ground, and yielded fruit, some an hundredfold, some sixtyfold, some thirtyfold.

MATTHEW XIII

The Sower

From the painting by Millet

PARABLE OF THE RICH FOOL

The ground of a certain rich man brought forth much fruit.

And he thought within himself, saying, What shall I do, because I have no room where to bestow my fruits?

And he said, This will I do: I will pull down my barns and build greater; and there will I bestow all my fruits and goods.

And I will say to my soul, Soul, thou has much goods laid up for many years; take thine ease, eat, drink, and be merry.

But God said unto him, Thou fool, this night thy soul shall be required of thee; then whose shall those things be which thou hast provided?

So is he that layeth up treasure for himself and is not rich toward God.

LUKE XII

PARABLE OF THE TARES

The kingdom of heaven is likened unto a man that sowed good seed in his field.

But while men slept, his enemy came and sowed tares among the wheat, and went his way.

But, when the blade was sprung up and brought forth fruit, then appeared the tares also.

So the servants of the man came and said unto him, Did'st not thou sow good seed in thy field? From whence then hath it tares?

He said unto them, An enemy hath done this.

The servants said unto him, Wilt thou then that we go and gather them up?

But he said, Nay; lest while you gather up the tares, ye root up the wheat with them.

Let both grow together until the harvest; and in the time of harvest, I will say to the reapers, Gather ye together first the tares and bind them in bundles to burn them; but gather the wheat into my barn.

MATTHEW XIII

Gather the wheat into my barn.

MOSES TO THE CHILDREN OF ISRAEL

The Lord thy God bringeth thee into a good land, a land of brooks of water, of fountains and depths that spring out of valleys and hills.

A land of wheat and barley, and vines and fig trees and pomegranates; a land of olive and honey;

A land wherein thou shalt eat bread without scarceness; thou shalt not lack anything in it; a land whose stones are iron, and out of whose hills thou mayest dig brass.

When thou hast eaten and art full, then thou shalt bless the Lord thy God for the good land which he hath given thee.   DEUTERONOMY VIII

Thou shalt bless the Lord.

A THANKSGIVING

For flowers that bloom about our feet,
For tender grass so fresh, so sweet;
For song of bird and hum of bee,
For all things fair we hear or see;
   Father in heaven, we thank Thee.

For blue of stream and blue of sky,
For pleasant shade of branches high;
For fragrant air and cooling breeze,
For beauty of the blooming trees;
   Father in heaven, we thank Thee.

—Ralph Waldo Emerson

Frankfort, Ky.,
Nov. 25, 1915.

Dear Friends:

This little book was written especially for the dear boys and girls of the moonlight schools, not the youngest, perhaps, but the finest school children on earth.

You have set a fine example for both young and old, and one which many will surely follow.

You have been faithful and have finished the first of the series of Country Life Readers. The second is now ready for you, and the author hopes that you will read it with profit and pleasure.

The world has great need of men and women who read well and write well. These are two of the greatest arts, and remember that they can be acquired only by constant practice.

The preparation of this book has been truly a labor of love. If you have received any benefit from it, the author is fully repaid.

Yours sincerely,

CORA WILSON STEWART.

THE ALPHABET

a	A	*a*	a	*n*	N	*n*	n
B	B	*b*	b	*O*	O	*o*	o
C	C	*c*	c	*P*	P	*p*	p
D	D	*d*	d	*2*	Q	*q*	q
E	E	*e*	e	*R*	R	*r*	r
F	F	*f*	f	*S*	S	*s*	s
G	G	*g*	g	*J*	T	*t*	t
H	H	*h*	h	*U*	U	*u*	u
I	I	*i*	i	*V*	V	*v*	v
J	J	*j*	j	*W*	W	*w*	w
K	K	*k*	k	*X*	X	*x*	x
L	L	*l*	l	*Y*	Y	*y*	y
M	M	*m*	m	*Z*	Z	*z*	z

[90]

WORD LIST

(To be used for spelling)

ache	blade	·buy	cot	ears
add	bless	cakes	could	ease
air	bloom	came	cows	eye
all	blue	can	crime	fair
and	boil	care	crop	fall
are	book	cast	cut	fat
as	bought	changed	cup	fed
at	box	cheats	date	feed
bad	boys	check	day	feet
bake	brass	child	dead	fell
ball	break	choked	deep	field
bank	breathe	clean	depths	figs
barn	breeze	closed	did	fill
beans	bring	cloth	dirt	filth
be	broil	club	does	fire
bed	brook	cold	done	first
been	brought	come	down	floods
bees	Brown	cooked	drink	foe
best	brush	cool	drop	fold
big	build	coop	dry	food
bind	burn	corn	each	fool
bird	but	cost	earth	for

forth	had	if	like	much
four	hard	in	lives	mud
fowls	has	is	lodge	mush
fresh	have	it	long	must
fried	he	Jane	looks	my
friend	hear	John	Lord	name
from	heard	Jones	lose	nay
fruit	helps	joy	loss	near
full	hens	juice	love	neat
gave	her	just	low	needs
get	herbs	keep	made	news
girls	hers	kept	make	nice
give	hewn	kill	man	night
glad	hill	kind	mark	no
God	him	know	mash	nod
good	his	lack	may	not
got	hold	laid	meal	now
grains	holes	land	mean	nuts
grass	home	large	meat	of
gray	hot	last	men	off
great	hours	learned	milk	oil
green	house	left	missed	old
ground	how	less	moist	on
grow	hum	lest	more	one
half	hurt	let	most	or

ought	raise	shall	sown	takes
our	read	she	space	tan
out	red	should	spark	tares
pain	rid	show	spoil	taste
paint	right	sick	sponge	team
part	ripe	sieve	spoon	teeth
pay	rise	sign	spray	tell
pen	road	six	spread	ten
pigs	rob	skin	spring	test
pint	rope	sky	sprung	than
pipe	root	slept	stalk	thank
place	rules	slops	stamp	that
plan	runs	small	stand	the
please	same	smell	start	thee
plants	save	smile	steal	them
plowed	say	soaks	stewed	their
polls	schools	soft	stock	then
pone	scorched	soil	stone	there
poor	scrub	some	stop	these
pour	see	son	store	things
price	seeds	soon	stream	thine
prize	seems	soul	strong	think
pure	seen	soup	such	third
put	sell	South	sun	this
rain	shade	sow	sweep	thought

thorns	try	we	white	work
thou	tub	weeds	who	worn
thread	turns	week	whose	worth
three	two	well	why	would
thy	up	went	wife	write
till	use	were	wild	wrong
time	voice	wet	will	yard
tire	vote	what	wilt	yarn
to	walk	wheat	winds	years
too	want	when	wise	yeast
train	was	whence	wish	yes
tree	washed	where	wood	you
tried	waste	which	words	young
true	way	while	wore	your

---

a bout	a mong	be cause	bun dles
a cre	an y	bed room	but ter
af fairs	ap peared	be fore	care less
a fraid	a way	be ing	cat tle
aft er	ba by	be stow	chil dren
a gain	bar ley	bet ter	cli mate
a go	bat ter	Bi ble	col or
al ways	beau ty	branch es	com pare
a mount	be came	buck ets	cor rect

cor rupt	fod der	la zy	pas ture
cot ton	fool ish	let ter	peo ple
coun try	for est	lik en	per son
de cay	forth with	lit tle	pick led
deep ness	foun tains	luke warm	plant ed
des sert	fra grant	lum ber	pleas ant
de stroy	Fri day	man y	poor er
de voured	gath er	mem ber	pre pare
di gest	go ing	mer ry	pret ty
din ner	gul lies	mois ture	pre vent
dirt y	har vest	Mon day	pud ding
dis ease	heav en	mon ey	rail road
dodg er	him self	moth er	reap ers
dol lars	hoe cake	muf fin	rel ish
ear ly	hon or	mus tard	re quired
eas y	hon ey	neith er	rich est
eat en	hors es	nev er	rip ens
en joy	hunt er	noth ing	roast ed
ev er	in to	of ten	rob bers
e vil	i ron	ol ive	ro tate
farm er	jack ets	on ly	sal ad
fa ther	Je sus	o pen	scarce ly
fi ber	king dom	oth er	scarce ness
fig ures	la bor	o ver	serv ants
flow ers	lay eth	own er	shad ow

shel ter	sus tain	to ward	wag on
shift less	ta ble	treas ure	Wednes day
shoot eth	tax es	Tues day	wee vil
show er	ten der	ug ly	win dow
sick le	there fore	un der	with ered
si lo	this tles	un til	with in
sleep ers	thou sand	un to	with out
sug ar	Thurs day	val leys	wom an
sum mer	tim ber	ver y	wom en
Sun day	tooth brush	wag es	yield ed

---

an oth er	hun dred fold	six ty fold
dif fer ent	news pa per	ta ble spoon ful
e lec tion	of fi cer	thir ty fold
en e my	pom gran ates	to geth er
ev er y	po ta toes	us u al ly
fam i ly	pro vid ed	veg e ta bles
hom i ny	Sat ur day	where un to